W. Shakespere
GENT.

D0392168

HiS ACTUAL NOTTEbooKE

SELF PORTRAIT
by
W. Shakespeare → (GENT.)

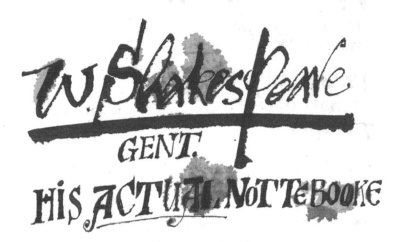

W. Shakespeare

GENT.

HIS ACTUAL NOTTEBOOKE

Together
WITH NUMEROUSE
ILLUSTRATIONS & ANNOTATIONS
BY
VERY
The Same Handde

ONLY TO BE
DISCOVERED & AUTHENTICKATED
BY
Graham Clarke ESQ:
400 YRS. LATER
of ye
EBENEZER PRESS

EBENEZER PRESS

White Cottage, Boughton Monchelsea,
Maidstone, KENT ME17 4LF

FIRST PUBLISHED 1992
© Graham Clarke 1992
Text Lettering & Pictures © Graham Clarke 1992

A CIP Record (whatever that is) is available from the British Library apparently.

ISBN 0 9502357 25

Produced in association with Pardoe Blacker Publishing, Lingfield SURREY.
Distributed in association with Windsor Books International, OXFORD.

This book is DEDICATED too.

& It is very nicely printed in SUNNY ITALY by NEW INTERLITHO S.p.A. MILAN.

CONTENTS
of Ye BOOKE.

continued overleaf ———→

CONTENTS CONT'D.

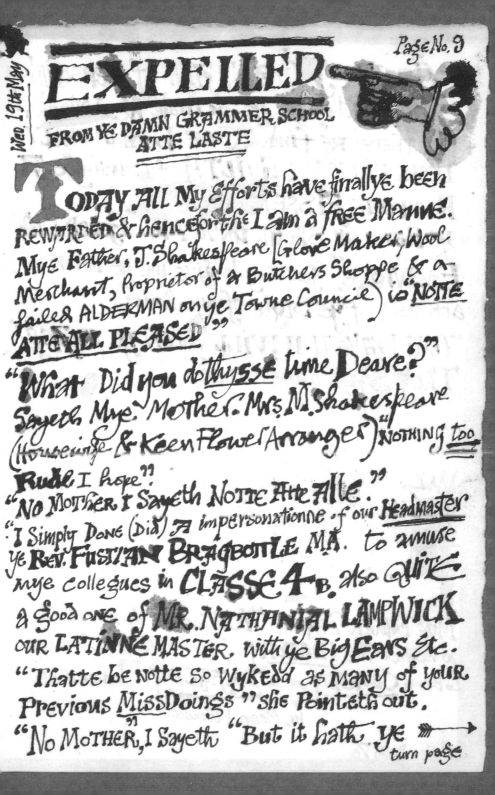

EXPELLED

FROM YE DAMN GRAMMER SCHOOL ATTE LASTE

TODAY ALL MY Efforts have finallye been REWARDED & henceforthe I am a free Manne. Mye Father, J. Shakespeare (Glove Maker, Wool Merchant, Proprietor of a Butchers Shoppe & a failed ALDERMAN on ye Towne Councie) is "NOTTE ATTE ALL PLEASED"

"WHAT Did you do thysse time Deare?" Sayeth Mye Mother. Mrs M. Shakespeare (Housewinfe & Keen Flower Arranger) "NOTHING too Rude I hope"

"No Mother, I Sayeth NOTTE Atte Alle."

"I Simply Done (Did) A impersonationne of our Headmaster ye Rev. FUSTIAN BRAGBOTTLE M.A. to amuse mye collegues in CLASSE 4-B. also QUITE a good one of MR. NATHANIAL LAMPWICK our LATINNE MASTER. with ye Big Ears Etc.

"Thatte be notte so Wykedd as Many of your Previous MissDoings" she pointeth out.

"No MOTHER, I Sayeth "But it hath ye →
turn page

GREAT AVANTAGE of PERSONALye affecktinge ye actuale headMaster"
He therefore findeth me both UTTERLY DESPICKABLE & GUILTY of Causinge A RIOTOUS ASSEMBELLYE.
Ye Boys all Shout UNTO ME "GOOD OLDE EarWigge," (for they do give me ye NAME on accounTe of ye Style of mye hair)
"ONE DAYe YOU WILL go ON YE STAGE." They Say. (GOODE IDEA)

REV. FUSTIAN BRAGBOTTLE M.A.

Mye Father Sayeth "William, I do NOTTE Know whether the HISTORY of your life will turn out to be a COMEDY or a TRAGEDY." * What does he Mean I Wonder?

* See Page 70

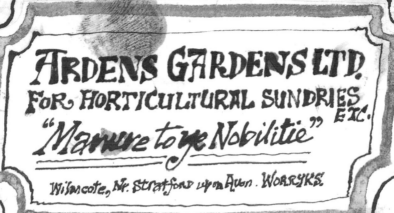

ARDENS GARDENS LTD.
FOR HORTICULTURAL SUNDRIES ETC.
"Manure to ye Nobilitie"

Wilmcote, Nr. Stratford upon Avon. WORRYKS.

Mother suggests I gette a Jobbe, or "GAINfulle Employment" As she do PREFER to call itte.

"Go and talke to your GRANDfather ARDEN" she telleth me "He be verrie fond of you thou knowest."

Not fond enough it seemeth, for when I go to see him concerninge mye future he is less than keen to offer me a position wythe hys company. He hath notte forgott ye INCIDENTE wyth ye CARTLOAD of HORSES DOINGS for her Ladyshyppe at ye MANOR HOUSE. apparentleye. "Do what you lyke boy," he belloweth, "Butte for GODDE's sake DON'T do it NOWHERE NEAR ME!" I take ye HINTE & a shillinge from ye CASH BOX.

WAY OUT

WITH MUCH RELUCTANCE I am going to have to WORK for MYe father. atte Leaste for ye time Beinge until Something better presenteth itseiffe.

My Father wisely decideth that I am "not cut out "To become a glove maker & too "WOOLY Headed" To buy and sell FLEESES for HIM. "You can make your self usefulle atte ye BUTCHERS Shoppe Boy, he Stateth & "Don't giveth Me noTrubble"

Thus commenceth my brieffe Careere as A BUTCHERS DELIVEReYE BOY & I am a bitte cut uppe about IT. Apparentlye I am to Carrye a DAMN GREATTE Baskette of SAUSAGES & HAMS & Suchlyke all about ye Towne for three FARTHINGes per FORTNIGHT (If I give No TRUBBALL)

I LYKE Thysse JOBBE, Muche
for Moste of OURE ESTEEMED
CUSTOMERRES ARE ITTE SEEMETH
Actuale Pubblik Houses, INNs, & All
SUNDRYE other such ESTABLISHMENTs
CONCERNED WITH ye BUSYNESSE of
DISPENSINGE QUANTITYES of ALE
lown ye ACTUAL TROATS of thirsty
TOWNSfolk, & ye Parched Travellers
(which do Abounde inn these Partes).

Thyrsty actuale Worke Thisse" I sayeth.
Deliveringe SAUSAGES & Suchlyke."
ALThough usuallye I gette offered a mugge
fWATER (to which I am ALLERGICKT)
SoMETIMES IT BE ALE To Which I
AM Parshall. I sooNE Discover Whyche
Landlords, Cookes & BarMaidds are Ye
MoSte OBLIGINGE in Thisse Matter &
I MAKE CERTAYNE they Recieve Ye
SAUSAGES CONTAININGE A Bit LESSE
Sawduste as a gesture of Good Will.

THUS I HAVE BECOMME WELL ACQUAYNTED WITH ALL YE TAVERNES OF YE TOWNE

& atte an EARLYER AGE thanne YE MIGHTE. otherwyse EXPECKTE.

MORE GOODE NEWS

Now I am furnished with a verry nice littel hand cart and can putte aside ye damn basket. GOODE.

FAMILY BUTCHERS

ON ye Jobbe

CONCERNING YE SUBJECKTE of SAILORS

AN ANCHOR.

ALL We do seem to hear about Nowadays is sailors. Sailors, Sailors, sailors. SIR. FRANCIS DRAKE, SIR Wotsit RALEIGH, SIR. SOMebody HAWKINS. Mye LORDs EFFINGHAMME & BLINDINGHAMME, Able Seaman Malachi Harbottle Etc. Etc.

GOODE IDEA

They do seem to be able to "catch the eye" of LADEYES ESPECIALLYE our QE NO 1. WE UNDERSTANDE [May GODDE BLESS HER, & ALL Who SAIL IN HER.] ETC.

Itte SEEMETH to ME (& SOME of ye other lads in ye "BLOATER & SKYROCKET" it's best BECOME A FAMOUS SAILOR, (SMELLY GANG of Ruffians Thatte they be.) TO GETTE ON IN ye World.

P.15

A Souvenier »»→
of
Mye Dayes as Deliverye
~~Boy~~ Personne.

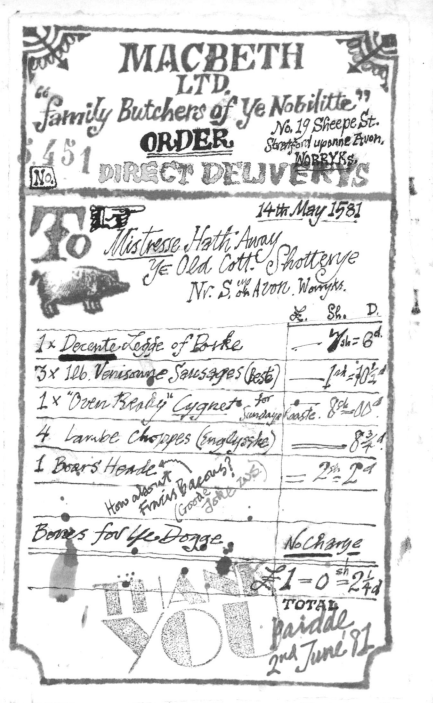

MACBETH LTD.

"Family Butchers of Ye Nobilitie"

ORDER

No. 19 Sheepe St.
Stratford uponne Avon,
WARWYKs.

№ 451

DIRECT DELIVERYS

14th May 1581

To Mistresse Hath'Away
Ye Old Cott. Shotterye
Nr. S. on Avon. Warwyks.

	£.	Sh.	D.
1 × Decente Legge of Porke		7sh =	6d.
3 × 1 lb. Venisonne Sausages (Beste)		1sh =	10½d
1 × "Oven Ready" Cygnet for Sundaye Roaste.		8sh =	11d
4 Lambe Choppes (Englysshe)			8¾d
1 Boar's Heade		2sh =	2d

How about Fryars Bacon? (Goode Joke this!)

Bones for Ye Dogge	No Charge	

£1 = 0sh = 2¼d

TOTAL

Paidd 2nd June '81

Page No. 17

As I was deliveringe ye actuale ESTEEMED ORDER to ye old cott. atte Shotterye Today (FRI. 13th March) a verrye strange lookinge person suddenlye appeared atte ye doorwaye. It was a femaile person I believe & weareth glasses.*

I doffeth my hatte & she spotteth my bald head. "Hatte actuale WORK. I should imagine" she sayeth, "DELIVERYNGE ye actuale Saugages & suchlike, would'st thou like a DRINK?"

DOTH she refer I WONDER, to WATER, Wine OR Ale?

"Of Ale" she sayeth promptly, before I even asketh.

Itte is verrye warm in ye Kitchen & she encourageth Me to remove Mye Hatte ETC.

She Looketh atte me a bitt funnie......

Hatte →

* Iffe these are notte invented yette they soon will be.

W.S. (GENT.)

ANNE OLD COTTAGE ATTE SHOTTERYE
(NR. STRATFORD UP ON AVON)

Whenever I am performing mye VOLUNTERRY
Worke of helpinge ye Lord of ye Manor look
after his VERRIE FINE HERD of DEERS I
always take withe me my ARTISTTES BAGG.
If accosted by ye Damn Bayliffe (as do
occsionnallie do happen) I gette out mye
LITTEL BOX of PAINTS and open mye Notte
BOOKE at a picture of Ye MOON *

Verrie Similar to Thysse

"I am butte a poor & totally innocent
ARTISTTE your HONNOR ship" I Say.
"& Thysse here be not a Bow & Arrow at all
BUTTE a special nightime SKETCHYNGE
EASEL of mye own inventionne.
"Pulle ye other one mate its gotte bells on"
HE do usuallye say as he buffets mye ear.

W.S. GENT. ✱

Propper Artisttes
are rather partial
to a nice Moon.

ye ACTUAL MOON

Called Inn at to "Ye Fig & Handcart" a TAVERN atte ye far end of Church Streete. I am on BUSYNESSE' (actuallye investign finding out whether their is a 'MARKET' for QUALITYE VENISON) As I quaffe Mye ALE I say in a MOSTE Casuale Manner.   Thusly.

"LandLORD, Wouldst thou be att all INTERESTED in a decent haunch OR Two of TopQUALITYE VENISON by any Chance? Cheap."

"I WOULD NOT Purchase a DEAD RAT FROM This GLABROUS TOXOPHILYTE" sayeth a voice FROM Ye GLOOM of ye Saloone BAR.

There SMIRKETH F.BACON & Thatte Chri-STOPHER Marlowe, Looking LIKE a Pair of SMOKED HADDOCKS with their stupid 'tobacco smokinge Pipes' & grinning fizzy-gwanys.

I tipp a QUART of BROWN ALE down ye front of BACONS BREECHES and walke out.

"AND You WILL come to a STICKY END Too MISTER Marlowe" I sayeth as I go.

NOTE:- Also I am going to obtain A actual WORD DICTIONARYE. W.S. (GENT)

Ye olde ~~woman~~ Lady in Ye Bridge Street Pie Shoppe sayeth kindly.

"One Daye Master Willyam me you will be really famouse, make no mystake"

"Thankyou INDEED" old MOTHER Twerford sayeth (quite POLITE) I intend to be verrie famous as a writer of Sonnets, plays etc. & as a probable collaborator (with others) of several & numerous dramatic works of possibble uncertain Authorship.?"

"Oh" sayeth ye ignorante olde woman "I didn't mean famous for ye Wrighting of plays & suchlyke, butte for eating such quantityes of mye beste pies & even NOT bothering to pay for themme."

What a Awfulle Way to ENCOURAGE ye Arts.

"Look here" old MOTHER Twerford sayeth I, how would you like to purchasse a decente bit of venison on the cheap?"

W.S.

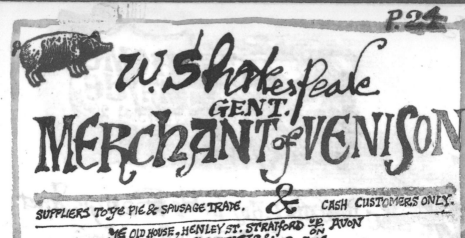

W. Shakespeale
GENT.
MERCHANT of VENISON

SUPPLIERS TO YE PIE & SAUSAGE TRADE. **&** CASH CUSTOMERS ONLY.

YE OLD HOUSE, HENLEY ST. STRATFORD UP ON AVON
WORRYKShire. ENG.

"**M**ye card Madam", sayeth I handing her mye actuale busynesse Card (As above) "it's your lucky daye and no Mystake." "Do Yourselffe a favour and take advantage of our fore-seasonne price. She placeth a REASONABLE order. But Refuseth to COUGH up **CASH** in Advance.

a damn shame actually as I was planninge to go out with ye Laddes TONIGHT: "Instead I Will do a Little VOLUNTERRYE WORKE" in MYE LORDS DEERE PARK.

As ye PIGGE opposite

AUTHORS
NOTE

I am not atte all pleased. A small RED PIGGE hath Presented himself atte sundrie & various places in thysse mye verrie PERSONAL BOOKE. I knoweth NOTTE (atte YE MOMENT) how he actuallye arriveth butte I will finde out. W.S. (GENT.) You can be sure.

PERSONAL.

I AM MOSTE RELIABLYE INFORMED (by a couple of ye Ladds in YE "NIMBLE RODENT" PUBLICK house IN Chapel Lane) thatte YE WOMAN called Hathaway who dwelleth in YE OLDE COT. atte SHOTTERE YE haveth "A BITTE of a Thinge" about menna wyth a shortage of actuale hair on the top of their heads. Apparently she do fancieth Me. I have accordingly VISITED ye actuale Hys n' Hers Hair Dressers JULIET & ROMEO to seek Some actuale hair RESTORER* Atte six greals for A rather SMALLE BOT'TLE This should be GOODE Stuffe.

* GOODE IDEA

23RD. APRIL

Mye ACTUAL BIRTHDAYE todaye. OUT With YE Ladds, Ben Johnson (No Actual 'H' apparentlye), Baldrick Fishtonsil, Dicky Burbage & ye reste of owR DARTES TEAM from ye BLOATER & SKYROCKET we have a match Against ye 'FIG & HANDCART' Tonight. No doubt F. Bacon will be PERFORMYNGE With his usuale UTTER Lack of SKILL & Ability to put his hand in his actuale PURSE Whenne its his turn to pay for ye DRINKS. "Oh Dear Oh Me he sayeth," I appear to have COMMETH to YE Pub MINUS ANY FINANCIAL WHEREWITHALL." EVEN Christopher Marlowe getts a bit fed uppe & He's NOT famouse for PAYINGE for his DRINKS GOD KNOWS. (pardon)

The Hathaway Woman from Shotterye spotteth ME in YE High St. today & without thinkinge I foolishly RAISE My hatte. A Misstake I fear.

HAMLET

by W, Shakespeare GENT.

On Your WAY Home from YE PUBBE take 6 fresh HENNS EGGS from Your NEIGHBOURS HENN COOPE & picke a Nyce GENEROUSE handfull of hys PARSLEY Whenne you GETTETH HOME Cutte A goodly slice of HAM choppe itte SMALLE To prevent against Discomfort of Ye BOWELS (pardon) DURING Ye Night, & Fryye in a QUANTYTIE of GOOSE DRIPPYNGE UNTIL LIGHTLY BROWNED. ADD Your 6 eggs & Thrash ye Lot together wythe Much Goode pepper & some SALT & also Your PARSLEY!

Do NOTTE Cooke for Too Long or Thysse Dysshe will be Muche Ruined. Eat Quicke

Chefs Tippe :— Take the Shells off Ye eggs.

A Typicalle Henne in ye actual egg Layinge Position

ONE of Mye Lighter Tasks as a BUTCHERS DELIVEREYE personne is to TAKE BUNDLES of feathers from our PLUCKINGE Shed To Mr. WM. CAXT'N Jnr. Jnr. These he doth actuallye Sell as hys SELECTED GENUINE GOOSE QUILLS "a fyrste Classe Penne atte a Moderate Price"

HALF A DOZEN for A GROAT (cheap)! SPECIALE OFFER!

INTERESTINGE FACTE
THE aforementioned premises DID ACTUALLYE SUPPLY, ALBEIT UNWITTINGLEYE this VERY NOTEBOOKE you KNOW HOLDIN your HANDE.

INK

W. CAXTON & SON LTD. EST. 1472

PRINTINGE PRESSE

This, very old Man who KEEPETH ye LITTLE PRINTER & STATIONEERS Shoppe in Tyler St. INFORMeth ME thatte hys actuale GRANDfather MORE oR LESS Discovereth ye ART of PRINTINGE, atte Leaste as far as thysse COUNTRIE is CONCERNED.

"VERRYE NYCE Too" I sayeth PRETENDYNGE TO BELIEVE him, "ANY chance of a Jobbe?"

"No SON" he sayeth "Thy spellinge be atrociousse & any-way I wisheth to END mye Days in PEACE."

Ye Badde News notte a great deal of luck with ye actualle HAIR RESTORER. "Keepe atte itte SIR" sayeth ROMEO atte ye Hairdressers & selleth me another Six Bottles.

Ye Goode News "See Opposyte" >>>———————>

SIR LUCUS BAMBOSH (ON STAGE)

"AS YOU LIKE IT

So Much Master William" Sayeth Goode
BREWER Mr. FLOWER "We are going
to stick your FIZZOG on ye actuale
BEER Labels."

What a honour. I will
Soon be famous NOW.

BEN (JONSON) sayeth wisely
"I can hardly imagine BLADDERWRAKS
puttinge F.BACON ESQ ON their LABELs
Eh Bill?" WE LAUGH.
(Bill & Ben FLOWERS top MEN.)

To Make A Nyce Stewwe of VENISON

Thysse Dysshe is Particularlye Economicalle iffe you are Able to steal all or some of ye Actual INGREEDYENTS.

"VENISON IS ALWAYS BEST POACHED" (JOKE)

[PRE-HEAT OVEN TO 180°C (350°F) GAS MARKKE 4.]

Avtiotique
Vignette 5
(actual
french)

Cutte ye Meate into 1 inch (one) Cubes & Duste in Seasoned * flour, fry up in some Butter nice & hotte. Pour into ye Cookinge Pottle a bottle (or several) of **RED WINE.** ALSO chuck in Some Nutmeggs, MACE, Some CLOVES, CINNAMON & CAYENNE Cooke for **2 HOURES** or until TENDER. pepper & Salt.

Water Cresses from Ye Avon will go well wyth thisse. (W.S. gent.)

AN ACTUAL POTATOE

(enlarged several times)

As brung t. ENGLAND bye thatte

SIR Walter Raleigh ~ Esq.

SO WE ARE TOLD.

inn 15$76 (og). GENT.

12.

MUCH ADDO ABOUT NOTHINGE

by W. Shakespeare GENT.

(ette)

ANOTHER Manne came into YE Pubbe at LUNCHTIME proudly bearing A POTATO. I bought itte in LONDON he sayeth, direct fromme SIR. W. RALEIGH & Co. (Novelties to HER GRACIOUS MAJESTY etc.) Itte cost me twelve GUINEAS (TRADE) a Bargain consideringe He sayeth. We inform himm it very much resembleth a **SPUD** the like of whyche we have GROWN & EATEN in thysse parte of WORRYKESHIRE for as long as anyboddye can remembbere, ROAST, FRIED, MASHED, BAKED & SAUTÉED (french) We have hadde YE lotte. We tell him

→ THE STRANGER thenne *departs* lookinge
MOST DISPLEASED & we ALL HAVE
A Jolly GOODE LAUGH.

ye damn BAYLIFFE catcheth Me again
'RED HANDED.'

YETTE ANOTHER PAINTINGE of YE DAMN MOON

W.S. GENT

TREATRICKLES

Itte Beinge Thursday Mye father W. Shakespeare Etc.
do 'spatch me on a mission.

"Proceed forthwith he say unto ye VERRIE
PLEASAUNTE littel Market Towne of CHIPPINGE
NORTON over ye border(s) in OXFORDShire.

Take TANTERMOUNT Ye Company's best Horse
& dont be late home...", he sayeth.

Thysse I do, AND ARRIVE atte ye said towne,
do mye Bussinnesse bye Noon & SUDDENLEYYE
feel moste verryie Thirstie. Therefore feel
obliged to PARTAKE of some modestte REFRESHMENTS in
YE OLD NAGGES HEAD PUBLYCKE HOUSE."
(NEXTE To YE MARKET SQUARE.)

⌐TODAYE IS Ye 27th of Febbuaryye¬

I EAT A VERRY DECENTTE porke Pie
(local) & quaff a meagre quartte of
he liquid they do refer to as As Ale hereabouts.

I THENNE SAY To ALL ASSEMBLED in Ye PUBLICKE
BAR. "In Exacktley 350 yrs. Time, chaps

Graham Clarke (sort of Artist) Will be

BORN in thysse TOWN. they all look atte me a
bitte funny & go on drinking their beer.
DON'T ACTUALLYE KNOW WHAT MADE ME SAY THYSSE] W.S.

A DISCOURSE UPONNE ye ACTUALE SUBJECKTE of DEERS & ye ACTUAL POACHING of ye SAME Writ Hereinafter for Ye Common Man. Etc.

(Page No. 40.) SORRY.

MYE LORD Thomas Lucy (SIR) onne hyse Estate atte Ye Charlecote (NEARBYE) hath a VERRIE FINE herd of fallow DEERS. (s) (plural)

We have GENERALLEY SPEAKINGE Two (2) Varieties (KINDS) of DEERE. ① Ye RED DEER (Verryie Popular in SCOTLAND Etc.) & ② YE Actual FALLOWE DEER (Ye REAL Thinge). I saye.

Mye LORD LUCY (as above) hath (haveth) ye FALLOWE as (we are pleased to contemplate). ROBIN HOOD Did Take GREAT INTERESTE in these fallowes & Itte is Mye Pursuit, Pleasure, & Possibilye Professione to do Lykewise.

TO BE CONTINUED (LATER)

See Page No. 46

I had only Juste Compleated my
VERRYE FYNE TOWNE MAPPE whenne
ye BayLiffs Damn Dog gotte into
Mye Bagge.

YE REMAINDER (s)

Towards ye
NORTHE

To BIRMINGHAM
(Note Lichfield)

KEY

S

E.

W.S.

Actual
Birthplace
of
W. Shakespeare
GENT. who was born here.
In ye yeare 1564

HENLEY ST.

Pub.

other pubs

To WARWICKE

"CAT &
FIDEL"

BIRMINGHAM
(notte Likely)

PUB

Alehouse

pub

GUILD STREET

HENLEY ST.

INN PUBS

TAVERNS

BRIDGE STREET

STREET

H ST.

SOME PUBS

RED LION COURTE

pubs

WATERSIDE

R.S.C.
Ratcatchers Social Clubbe

W

S

INN

pub

Eastwards

'ye Bloater & Skyrocket'
(PUB)

WARRICK

ye famous CLOPTON BRIDGE

3

2

1

SHEEPE STREET

ERRYE
arge

ub ese

TEN JOLLY GRAVEDIGGERS

PUBS

SOUTHERN LANE

YE LOVELYE RIVER AVON

Hotel

PUBS

BANBURY RD.

HOTEL & Pub

INN

CRICKETTE PAV.

LONDON ROAD
(To & fromme LONDON)

"MODUS ANACHRONOLOGIER" ©

PUB

YETTE MORE small RED pigges have
PRESENTED themselves in MY booke, I **WILL**
find out from whence they Commeth & wreak
A TERRYBALE REVENGE.

A Midsommer Night Stream by W. Shake speare. (ENT)

A Actuale Discourse uppon Ye Subjeckte of DEER POACHING CONT'D.

from Page No. 40 [of this Booke]

INCLUDINGE

A Poetic Tribute to ROBIN HOODE Esq:

Well Ye Actuale LATIN Name (as we say) for YOUR FALLOW DEER (s) is DAMA DAMA (Looke it uppe if THOU BELIEVEST ME NOT). THE MaLE ones are BUCKS NOTTE STAGS and in their first year (whenne they have butte Little horns) are called Prickets. Ye little deers are Fawns & Ye Ladye ones Does. Ye Jolly Olde MATINGE SEASON (pardon) is called RUTTING & taketh place in Ye AUTUMN of Ye YEAR. To BE CONT'D. (LATER)

⇉ Ye ROBIN HOOD POEM

I shall find Ye Sherriff of NOTINGHAMME In a alley dark & NARROW.
A shoot him Twixt his Legg & back with my LittLE Bow & ARROWE.
'Tis true I hunt Ye Sherriffs Deer but please Dont think ME BAD
I turn them into Sausagess in Memorye of Dad.
THE LORD the Knight the Squire say "These Sausagess are Nyce"
While Barmaids DAMES & SERVING Girls gette everything half-PRICE.
OUR Boots are GREEN our hats are GREEN our Tights are GREEN as well
AND WHENNE it RAINS the Dye comes out we're all as GREEN as HELL.

(pardon).

A POEM
Writ bye Me W.S. Gent.
in honour
of

Ben. Johnson

It being his Birthdaye.

I Like thisse bloke JONSON called Ben

Among the moste DECENTE of Menne

He be notte a STINKER

Like BACON (the Thinker)

& as DRINKER, Scores Ten out of TEN.

He telleth me he hath No 'L' in his JONSON butte "mindeth notte ye teossle".

I have given uppe all hope wyth ye hair
Restorer havinge NOTICED No IMPROVEMANT
Whattsoever after INVESTINGE in nearly 6
DOZEN BOTTLES of ye DAMN stuffe.

I meet GOODE MASTER ROMEO ONE LUNCHtime
IN YE BAT & DUMPLINGS TAVERNE in ye
High Streete and informe HIM (QUITE POLITE)
of ye ACTUALE facts of ye MATTER.

He seemeth Nor ye least interested & goeth on
CONVERSINGE wyth YE BARMAYDE TITania
Whenne he Disappeareth to YE GENTS (pardon) I tippe
the LAST half BOTTLE into his BEER.
(This you Might call gettinge your OWN back.)

                                    JOKE
                                    W.S.

Will have to CONSYDER A Wigge I suppose
   but withe GREAT RELUCKTANCE.

I first telleth mye Father that I wish to do PLAYWRIGHTINGE for mye Jobbe, TODAY (TUES. 14th)

Then you Will have to learn to SPELLE PROPPER(LY) he sayeth.

I saye cleverly, "FATHER Plays are to be saidde NOTTE read" butte he understandeth notte I fear.

I Belive My Father is whatte clever dick F. Bacon would call a "RIGHT OLDE FILLESTYNNE" (I heard him use thysse deadly insult MOSTE FREQUENTT whenne he doth gette into ARGUMENTS & in Ye "TEN JOLLY GRAVEDIGGERS" in Chapel Lane.

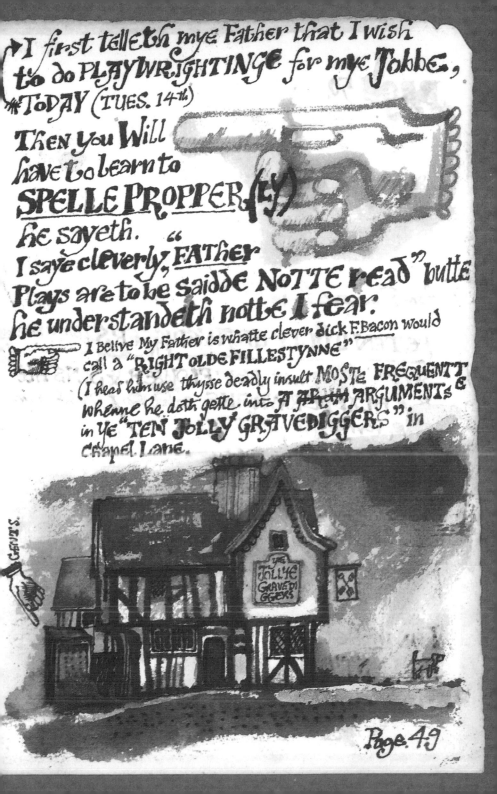

GAVE's.

THE JOLLYE GRAVEDIGGERS

Page 49

from Previous Page

YE TEN JOLLY GRAVEDIGGERS

Serveth **NOT FLOWER & SONS ALE**
But **BLADDERWRAKS** so we don't Drink in
there if we can avoid IT.

I am unable to fynde ye actuale WORD
FILLESTYNNE inn Mye NEW WORD
DICKTIONARRYe.

THE CHAUCERBURYE CART FARCE

Writ by W. Shakespeare GENT.

&

(Some of ye lads at Ye Pubbe.)

GRUBBUD BRITANICUSS

A MOST WITTIE & PLEASANT COMEDIE

DRAMATIS PER~~SO~~SONN'EAE (People in the actual play)

(Lattin). NOT IN ORDER of APPEARANCING

Septimus Quigley	A Merchant
Rufus Spratling	A Smart Young Lad (hero)
Molly	A Barmaid Etc.
Rev. Fustian Bragbottle	A Vicar.
Nathanial Lampwick	A Schoolmaster
Gurnard	A Villager
Scombroid	Another
King Henry VIII	the King Henry VIII.*

* Muste be a fat personne.

DRAMATIS PERSONNÆE (CONT'D.)

Sir Lucas Bambosh . . . . A Souldier

Tantermount . . . . His horse

Six Thousand foot Soldiers . . . . A Army

~~Frans~~ Francis Bacon . . . . A Buffoon

Thomas Gotchgutt . . . . A Gorbelly

John Gorbelly . . . . A Gotchgutt

Lady Tankerton Foxtonsil . . . . A Ladyye.

Land Lord of "Ye Badger & Firebucket" . . . . Ditto.

GRAND WIZARD of Ye MOSTE
VENERABLE ORDER of MASTER
HORSE & UNICORN VARNISHERS . . . . A Personage
(NON SPEAKINGE PARTE)

BARON Phylelwerichede Phyeltheriche . . . . AGENT.RY

JOHNATHAN POPE . . . . POPE JOHN.

PERSONAL NOTE.
Ye Parte of RUFUS SPRATLING (hero) XX is probablye ye
best ~~performede~~ performed by Myselfe Consideringe.
                                                        W.S.

YE ACTUAL PLAYE
ACT 1 No. (ye fyrste)

SCENE ONE
Ye action taketh place in "YE BRACE of TROLLOPS" a Nyce LITTLE ALEHOUSE at "CANTERBURRYE" in ye COUNTIE of KENT.

ENTER
SEPTIMUS QUIGLEY, REV. FUSTIAN BRAGBOTTLE, GURNARD, SCOMBROID & HENRY VIII.

QUIGLEY "What will you have then lads?"

ALL "A Pint of FLOWERS* if it's all the same to you Squire."

QUIGLEY "A Pint of FLOWERS* all round if you please Luv."

— *(She pulls FIVE pints of ALE)

MOLLY "That'll be exactly TEN GROATS please Sir."

(QUIGLEY GIVES her A TEN GROAT PIECE)

QUIGLEY (winking atte ye lads) "KEEP the Change Darlin'."

MOLLY (Yawning) "Thankyou Sir very nice I'm sure."

ENTER RUFUS SPRATLING (hero)

(he speaks).
"Hark well Ye Ye Wamblinge CORNCRAKE Wythe his Crisp & beauteous croakes
AND Your skulkinge NIGHTINGGALE whos Evening Scroops full RENT Ye Evening Eal

Hark too Your Merry FROGGE who gurgs his ploppish
tunes ^with mawkishe lust & baleful Threnody. *full so

AND Your noble GARDEN WORM who MAKES No
TUNE atte alle butte mimes his play RIGHT NOBLY
Consideringe He hath no legge nor eye & little schooling
in ye Arts. Liste well unto these fearless PROMULGATION
for these Mye present utteringes are MOST PHILOSOPHICALL
& SAGE.

GURNARD (he speakes) Erm.....

RUFUS SPRATLING
If thou believest, goodish Gurnard thou canst do
BETTER, consider the Joyous BLOTTER, the
NOBLE KIPPERS UNCLE . WELL done I SAY. Oh
Piscine HERO & true Englishmanne, FEAR-
Less as a Brand New Chimney Brush
& thrice as witty as a frenchmans Eartrumpet *
(He has a quicke swigge from HENRY VIII's ALE
TANKARD)

GURNARD (he speakes againe) "Ermm... .. .."

RUFUS SPRATLING "I thanke thee brave
Gurnard for thy welcome interferences
                        moste

* I might change thysse bit later. W.S.   Page 54

Thou Art as wise as thou Art BEATIFUL,
IF PERCHANCE....."

HENRY VIII (Interrupteth)
"Would you fancy a drink Rufus lad
it's mye actual ⟶ round."

RUFUS SPRATLING
"Cheers your Magniloquent Corpulence?"

Six Thousand foot SOLDIERS
"Thankes Squire I'll have a swifte half of
FLOWERS ALE if its all the same to you"

HENRY VIII. (lookinge surprised)
"Where did that lotte come from thenne?"

W. Shakespeare "Sorry Henry I forgotte
to say ENTER SIX Thousand Foot Soldiers etc.
write   Artists lysenase etc. you know.

MOLLY (Servinge Six Thousand ½ PINTS) ALE)
(She speaks to Rev. Fustian Bragbottle)
"Quite busy Tonight Eh Vicar?"

ye END of SCENE ONE ... EXEUNTE ⟶

CONT'D.

❋ Goode Choice.

ACT No. 2. (YE SECOND)

SCENE 1.

Ye action taketh place in "YE BADGER & FIREBUCKET" a PUBLICKE HOUSE JUSTE OUTSIDE YE WALLS of YE CITY of ROCHESTER in YE SAME SAID COUNTIE of KENT.

ENTER SIR LUCAS BAMBOSH RIDING his HORSE **TANTERMOUNT**. & OTHERS

LANDLORD "SORRY GUV'NOR NO HORSES IN YE PUBLICK BAR" (he points to a sign)

EXIT SIR. LUCAS BAMBOSH RIDING HIS HORSE **TANTERMOUNT**.

SCENE 2

Ye ACTION etc. YE SAME. (as above). BUTTE A butte Later.

ENTER GOTCHGUTT, GORBELLY & FRACIS BACON, he carrys A Large Codfysshe in an offensive MANNER. •

GOTCHGUTT (he speaks) "What's It To be thenne LADDES?"

GORBELLY "I'll have a PINT of the usualle please Gotchy."

GOTCHGUTT "How about you then Frank?"

F. BACON "What?"

GOTCHGUTT "Would you like a DRYNKE!" [A butte EXASPER-ATEDDE.

F. BACON THANKYOU THOMAS, MOSTE KINDE of YOU. I WOULD LIKE A ......

ENTER RUFUS SPRATLING (hero), Lady Tankerton Foxtonsil, & OTHERS.

SPRATLING (speaking & pointing his finger atte FRANCIS BACON) "Beholde Thysse **CORPUS PORCUS** friends & Its **GAWKISH** structure. Where limb & whatever Brain it hath DONT Marry uppe Too Smart, HE is COCHONIQUE BEYONDE the 'Maginings of ART." [laughter]

F. BACON (continuinge hys previous speeche) "...HALF PYNT of BROWN ALE & **7** GERKINGE Please Good Master GOTCHGUTT."

GOTCHGUTT "Half a pint of your cheapest Brown Ale & a pickled Wotsit LANDLORD" iffe You'd Be so kinde."

LANDLORD "CERTAINLYE SIR HALF A Pint of BROWN ALE & A NICE Bigge Pickled GERKINGE Coming uppe Right away"

SPRATLING (Maste Wittie) "Twill probablye Come uppe againe Later Knowing our FRANK" [Nearly Everyone Laugheth with Much veritable Jocosity & PESIFLAGE]*

Ye END of SCENE TWO ACT 2.

* I am muche pleased wyth mye new DICKTIONARRIEE

What dost thou thynke of It so far?

ACT 3 (ye Thyrde Act)

SCENE ONE
ye action taketh place on BORD YE DUCHESS of
BUMPKINSHYRE (a shippe).

ENTER 👉 NAThanial Lampwicke, Gotchgut
GORBELLY, RALph STEADman,*
HENRY VIII (Parte 1), ELWYN
BLACKER,* Rufus SPRATLING &
OTHERS.

GORBELLY (speaking)
" It certainlye brings on a thirst lookinge at all
this SEAWATER".
ELWYN BLACKER "Thats Very kinde of you I'll have
a flagon of Malmsey please" (he swiggeth it
in one go). Mmmm..Verrye Nice & ye SWANNE
Casserole please with all ye trimmynges (as they say)
Butte so easye on ye actuale sprouts iffe you dont Mind.
RALPH STEADman. (he speaketh unto R. Spratlinge) (Thus:
" Is This SOME SORT of PLAY We're IN ?"
Rufus SPRATLING "Yes, I believe it Muste be."
RALPH STEADman (speakinge Againe) "Thank Ye Lord
I thought We might be Real for a MOMENT?"
          (GOODE STUFFE Thysse.)

---

* THESE Two PERSONS DO NOT APPEARE IN YE DRAMATIS
PERSONNAE ON PAGES Nos. 51 & 52. BUTTE NEVER MYNDE.
                                    W.S.(GENT.)

Rufus Spratling (adopting a theatrical posture)

"Persuest Notte faire CITIZENS ye paltrye
Garneringe of coin & currencey for **Thyself**
But make some Vertue of a gift on this occasionne.
Bestowe thy **FISCAL** gift & whereisitthat upon
some merry Quaffers of Ale, of merry Landlorde,
Hencethy generositie Till reach your honest
farmers Hops & Barley & een your Brewer
Moste Valiant & worshipfulle of Mortals. &
ALso these Actors. Give Moste Generously
Good Sirs Lest some "Minor Accident"
befall thee on thy way home.
"Cough Up **NOW**."

YE INTERVALE.

FLOWE
BEST
ALE

ALTHOUGH Thysse PLAY IS GOINGE REALLY WELL. I Thinke
perhaps I will Leave itte for ye **Tyme** Beinge.

W.S (GENT).

NOTES

APART FROM THE PIGGS THISS
BE A DAMN FVNE BOOKE

B. JONSON (Age 16)

I LYKE ITT.

OH
SORRY BILL
B.J.

IDEAS of MINE

FOR

Suggested INTERVALe Refreshments

"QUAFF'N SCOFFE Ltd"
No 29 BRIDGE ST. S^{up}_{on} AVON
Worrykshyre
ENGLANDE

GOODE IDEA

FLOWERS FYNE ALES.*
MRS. TWERFORDS EXCELLENTE PIES.
fresh Apricotts - ARDENS GARDENS LTD.
A Potatoe ROYALE surpryse ←
MACBETHS family SAUSAGES
BOILED BACON . . . . .

I should have putte
in a bit about KING EDWARD here eh?

I BELIEVE I have juste
WORKED OUT who Done DID
the ACTUALE PIGGES.

* Iffe all thysse free Advertisinge is'nt good for
A couple of pints I don't know what is.
                                    AUTHOR

YE DEER Poachinge Must be putte aside for A while as I have a Bitte of trubbal.

YE DAMN BAYLIFF APPREHENDETH ME again and stateth "This be the TWELFTH Night this year I have CAUGHT You on ye Jobbe you yong VILLAIN & This Time I am Taking You To SEE MY LORD LUCY he will give it To You good & PROPPER make No Misake"

I giveth him a brief Lecture upon ye evils of ye CLASS SYSTEM & Point out how dangerous itt can be To Buffet a young PERSONNE around ye ear. ALL to No AVAIL.

ACCORDINGGLYE I have taken uppe ye fisshynge as MY NEW NOCTIVAGOUS PERSUIT.

YE Lovelye RIVER AVON CONTAINETH A Abundance of FyNE fishes Butte they all apparentlye belonge To SomeBoddy ELSE.

THE SHYLOCK KEEPER NERVOUSLYE explaineth This Actuale fact to Me when he SPOTteth ye Tail of a SALMON Pokinge fromme My BAG, I offer HIM A POUND of FISH for NOT REPORTINGE ME to YE DAMN BAYLIFF.

BLACK SYDNEY

*Now Stuffed & on Display in ye Saloon Bar of Ye "Blaster & Skyrocket" BRIDGE St.

A VERRIE LARGE FYSSHE (A PYKE) INDEEDE

(49 lbs. 4½ oz.)

TAKEN FROM YE RIVER AVON with ROD & LYINGE By W.Shakspeare GENT.

"Wythe Considerable Difficultie."

YE LOVELY RIVER AVON

A WATER COLOUR PAINTING
by
W. Shakspere (GENT)

A Midsummer Night Mare

Last night I suffered A Moste TERRIBAL DREAM
Wherein Ye Hatfi-AWAY WOMAN ASKETH Mye E
Fathec foc Mye hande in MARRIAGE! & he sayeth YEA!

I VoW I Will NeveR eat CHEESE last thing atte
Night EVER AGAINNE.   W.S.

ye ROMANTICKLES

MYE DREAME has come TRUE!

I am actuaLLye **MARRYED** to THE WOMAN HATH-AWAY.

HER Name apparently is **ANNE** (I discover this duringe YE ACTUAL Church Service Luckily So Do NOTTE HAVE the Embarrssmente of askinge her on the way HOME).

"What shall WE call ye BABY thenne DARLINGE?" She sayeth.

"How about **TROILUS** iffe it's a boy & **CRESSIDA** iffe It's a Little gIRL." ? she suggesteth.

"**GORDON BENNET**" sayeth I.

"Thats Nice Dear" She smileth & what if its a LITTLE gIRL?"

"Oh Dear" "Oh Dear"
WS (GENT).

"What have you been up to then Will?"
Sayeth BEN JONSON (beste Manne)
Giving Me A Wicked Looking **KING LEAR**.

"**I** am to become a ACTUALE fatheR", sayeth I.

"Thenne you WILL Notte be playinge DARTS in ye
"Bloater & SkyRocket" so often I imagine" HE
STATETH somewhat despondant.

"I feaR, Notte BENJAMIN old chappe" Sayeth I
For ye Woman HATH.Away giveth Me stricte
INSTRUCKTIONS ON ye **SUBJECKT** of Ale.Houses
& Suchlike. HENCEForth & HENCEFifth I
WILL SPENd my EVENINGES **INN DOORES**
Writinge famous PLayS & Suchlike &
Most Likely SONNETS too I Imagine, what
with one thinge & Another."

A REALLY GOODE IDEA for AN ENTIRERLY NEW SORTTE of THEATRE

Ye Globe Artichoke Theatre

designed by W. Shakespeare GENT.

Alwayse Remember I done did thysse fyrste. WS

Page 69.

Goode News

COMEDIE & TRAGEDIE

OTHER NEWS

A MANNE in Ye BLOATER & SKYROCKET says we've Just Won the SPANISH ARMARDO MATCH (whatever that Might actuallye Be) & we should toast all ENGLISH SAILORS. "GOODE IDEA we saye OR BOIL them OR FRY them WE DONT CARE."

OURE MOST GLORYIOUS

QUEEN ELIZABETH

Ye Fyrste

YE ACTUAL Goode QUEEN BESS as she do wish to be knowne is to visit STRATFORD upon AVON Todaye. She TRAVELLETH to KENILWORTH we are Told & All stations NORTH Butte wisheth to make a 'FLYING VISITTE' to ye BLACK SWANN (Publicke House) in SOUTHERN LANE. No Doubt she wisheth "to Powder her Nose" etc, on her way uppe fromme LONDON. & try a swig of FLOWERS.

GOODE IDEA

Mye Plan is SIMPLE I WILL wait outside ye Pubbe until her carriage arriveth; as she alighteth I will "take a leaf" from SIR. W. RALEIGH (his booke) & Lay My cloak in a puddel. She will NO DOUBT be Maste imprest.

UNFORTUNATLYE

Whenne I carry out mye plan I recieveth Notte **A KNIGHTHOOD** (as I expeckteth) butte a funnye Look from **HER MAJESTY** and a clip arounde ye **EAR** from ye **COACHMANNE.**

(Juste Mye Luck, It hath notte rained for over SIX WEEKS)

"Whatte may one aske is Your Name Little Man?"

DEMANDETH YE ACTUALE QUEENE of ACTUALE ENGLANDE!

"W. Shakespeare (GENT.)" sayeth I, Doffinge ye hatte.

"Mmm..." she museth lookinge atte Me WITH INTERESTE

"& Whatte Might one aske do you gette Uppe to whenne Notte PRETENDINGE to be a famouse butte rather boringe SAILOR Like SIR WOTSIT RALEIGH?"

"I AM An ACTOR & WRIGHTOR of PLAYS Iffe it Pleaseth Youre GORGEOUS MaJesty" sayeth I

(Realinge I'm onto a goode thinge).

"Mmmm..." she Museth "Do You, May one enquire, ever fynde Yourself in London by any chance?"

"MMost FREQUENT ACTUALLYE Youre utter Royalnesse" sayeth I, are you keen then on ACTORS & Suchlike?"

⇒⇒⇒ →

"Especiallye Balde ones", She Sayeth
"Do Looke Me Uppe Sometyme Mr.
W̄ Shakespeare."
(GENT.)

A
Mrs. Shakespeare (formerly Ye Hathaway Woman) was
notte actuallye impressedde, "how do you like ye baby's new
bedroome curtains?" She enquireth.
"VERRY NYCE DEAR", I sayeth widely.

Whenne I am RICHE & FAMOUSE I INTENDE to BUILD a NYCE **NEW PLACE** PROBABLYE atte YE CORNER of CHAPEL ST. & CHAPEL LANE.

Thysse, MYE OWN designe I showeth to YE Hath-Away WoMan or (Mrs. W. Shakkespire Etc.) "Verrye Nyce Too she "sayeth & QUITE LARGE ENOUGH UNTIL "Ye RESTE of YE Kidds arrive." "ACTUALLY" She COMMENTETH "Itt RaTher RESEMBLETH a LOAD of Pubbs."

MORE TROUBBLE

Followinge ye variouse Diffyculties with ye VENISON BUSYNESSE & Mye Night Work with My LORD LUCYS SALMONS Etc. He declareth PUBLICKLY that I am NOT A MORAL PERSONNE & should BE NOT ALLOWED to ENTER any of ye INNS, PUBBES, TAVERNES, ALEHOUSES Etc & Likewise Establishments including HOSTELERIES of ye SAID TOWNE of STRATFORD up on AVON. & NOTICES to BE POSTED ACCORDYNGLY.

THE IMMORAL, BARRD fromme these Premises

BY ORDER

A LACK & A LASS
(of beer & ale)
(see opposite page)

TODAYE A TRAVELLINGE THEATRE came To THYSSE TOWNE PERCIVALE PILLOKE & his SEVERAL PERFORMYNGE PERSONS.

I Am Much Immpressed I MUCTE ADMITTE BY THESE TRAVELLING PLAYERS & MOST PARTICULARLYE BY YE WARDROBE MISTRESSE. I DONT KNOW EXACTLY her Actuale Jobbe BUT I look ForWARD to FINDINGE OUT on our way Down to LONDON TOWNE.

EXEUNT 👉